I Love Ponies...

Pony
Club

Sandy Ransford

QEB Publishing

Editor: Amanda Askew
Designer: Izzy Langridge

Copyright © QEB Publishing. Inc. 2011

First published in the United States in 2011 by
QEB Publishing, Inc.
3 Wrigley, Suite A
Irvine, CA 92618

www.qed-publishing.co.uk

Library of Congress Cataloging-in-Publication Data

Ransford, Sandy.
  Pony club / Sandy Ransford.
    p. cm. -- (I love ponies)
  Includes index.
  Summary: "Covers all the basics of what Pony Clubs do, from teaching
techniques to young riders and providing camps to setting up horse
riding competitions"--Provided by publisher.
  ISBN 978-1-60992-098-2 (library binding)
 1. Pony Club. 2. Ponies--Juvenile literature. 3. Horsemanship--Juvenile
literature. I. Title.
  SF310.A1R36 2012
  636.1'6--dc22

                        2011011398

ISBN 978 1 60992 098 2

Printed in China

Website information is correct at time of going to press. The publishers
cannot accept liability for the content of the Internet sites that you visit,
nor for any information or links found on third-party websites.

Picture credits
(t=top, b=bottom, l=left, r=right, c=centre, fc=front cover)
All images are courtesy of Bob Langrish images unless stated below.
Alamay 14tr David L. Moore – Oahu, 14br ableimages, 18br Kumar
Sriskandan
DK Images 7br Kit Houghton, 8 Dorling Kindersley, 10r Andy Crawford,
10l Kit Houghton, 11br Dorling Kindersley, 17tr Bob Langrish,
Shutterstock fc-r Groomee, fc-tl Lenkadan, 19tl cynoclub

Words in **bold** are explained in the Glossary on page 22.

Remember!
Children must always
wear appropriate clothing,
including a riding hat, and
follow safety guidelines
when handling or riding
horses and ponies.

Contents

Joining a Riding Club

Whether or not you have your own pony, you can have fun joining a riding club or a branch of The Pony Club. You will meet other children and their ponies, and learn a lot about riding and pony care.

The Pony Club

The United States Pony Club (U.S.P.C.), a program for youths, teaches riding, mounted sports, and the care of horses and ponies. There are Pony Club centers across the United States, so it should be easy to find one in your neighborhood. Other countries have their own versions of The Pony Club, too.

This young rider is wearing a Pony Club tie as part of her riding outfit.

Riding clubs often have their own premises, which will have a riding ring and jumps for you to practice going over.

Going to Meetings

Some branches of The Pony Club and some riding clubs hold meetings at riding schools, which means you can go along even if you don't have your own pony. They will let you handle and ride one of their ponies.

Indoor School

These riding club members are lucky to have the use of an indoor school for their classes. This means they can ride and do exercises in the saddle whatever the weather.

When you go to a meeting, an instructor will help you with your riding, and answer questions about pony care.

Going to Meetings

You may be lucky enough to live near the meeting place of your club, and be able to ride there. If not, you will need transport for your pony.

Transport

Ponies can travel in either a **horse truck** or a **horse trailer.** Sometimes you can share transport with a friend.

This truck can carry several horses or ponies.

Trailer Travel

A pony can travel in a two-horse trailer, like this one, either with or without the central partition in place. Some trailers also have side ramps, so you can lead the pony out forward to avoid you having to back it down the ramp to unload it.

This trailer can be pulled behind a car.

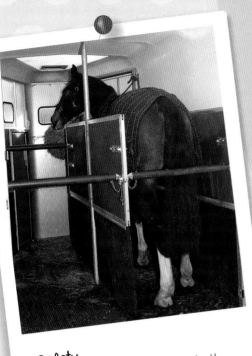

Into the Trailer

When you lead a pony into a trailer or truck, walk confidently straight up the ramp.

Safety

Ponies need to be tied on both sides when they are traveling to stop them trying to move around during the journey.

This horse is wearing a travel blanket, travel boots, and a tail wrap.

Protective Clothing

When a pony travels in a trailer or truck, it needs **travel boots** to protect its legs from knocks, and a tail wrap to prevent any rubbing. If you are not going far, it can travel with its **tack** on.

Learning More

When you go to meetings of The Pony Club or your riding club, you will learn a lot about ponies, including how to handle your pony and keep it healthy.

Top Tip!

Learn the parts of a horse so you know a forelock from a **fetlock**!

Parts of a Horse

It's important to know the correct names for the different parts of a pony's anatomy. Then you will know what people are talking about when they refer to them.

forelock

ear

crest

loins

withers

back

tail

cheek

nose

thigh

shoulder

chest

belly

knee

hoof

hock

fetlock

8

Pony Fitness

You can help a pony get in shape by gradually increasing the amount of exercise it takes, cutting down its grazing, and giving it more hard feed.

overweight, grass-fed pony

Fit pony

How to Lead a Pony

Lead your pony on its left side, with your right hand near its head and your left hand at the end of the line. Then, if needed, you can let go with your right hand and bring the pony around with your left hand.

Approaching a Strange Pony

Walk toward the pony's head from one side. Speak to it, allow it to sniff your closed fist, and pat it on the neck. That way the pony knows you are a friend.

Improving your Riding

At some of your riding club meetings you will learn exercises that will improve your riding and give you more confidence in the saddle.

Riding Without Stirrups

Riding on a longe line with your stirrups crossed over your saddle will help improve your seat in the saddle and your balance. If you feel insecure, hold on to the front of the saddle.

Riding Without Reins

Tying your reins and riding without them—called **longeing**—will also improve your balance when riding. The person holding the longe line will control the pony.

Riding without stirrups in trot is very bumpy! You have to learn to sit really deep in the saddle.

Exercises in the Saddle

There are a lot of exercises you can do while you are sitting on a pony as long as someone is holding it for you. The exercises will make you supple and give you more confidence.

Hold your arms out and twist around to each side from your waist.

Touching your Toes

Lift your right hand up in the air then bend down to touch your left foot. Straighten up, then repeat the exercise with your left hand touching your right foot.

Lying Back

Lie back until your head touches the pony's back. Try to sit up again without holding on to the saddle. If you can't, pull yourself up using the front of the saddle.

Working Harder

As your riding improves, you will learn more advanced exercises, and also how to handle problem ponies.

Making your Pony Move

Some ponies don't want to go forward. To encourage your pony, shorten the reins, squeeze hard with your legs, and say firmly "Walk on." If it still doesn't move, you can use a whip just behind the girth (the strap under the horse's belly) to reinforce your leg aid with a gentle tap.

Moving Too Quickly

Some ponies want to set off at great speed, especially when they canter. First of all, never lean forward, as this will make the pony think you want it to go faster. Keep your reins short and sit down in the saddle. If possible, try to ride the pony around in a circle to slow it down—but don't turn it too fast or it could fall over.

Working as a Pair

Riding around side by side with another pony is a good exercise in control. There are classes for riding in pairs at shows, and it's fun to do—though much more difficult than it looks. The ponies' heads should be level, and remember that when you turn, the pony on the outside has to move faster than the one on the inside.

Meet Up Fact!
Ponies ridden side by side may want to race each other if they canter.

When riding as a pair, it's easier if the larger pony is on the outside of the smaller one.

Pony Camp

For pony lovers who long to spend all day with ponies, pony summer camp is perfect. It's a chance to have a lot of fun with your friends and their ponies.

At the Camp

You will probably sleep in a tent, and your pony will be turned out with the others in a field. You will have to take care of your pony yourself, and also help with cooking meals and keeping camp tidy.

These ponies have had their morning ride and are resting before a class in the school later on.

My Pony Summer Camp Diary

7 a.m. I crawled out of my sleeping bag, got dressed, and went out to feed the ponies. It's a bright, sunny day—hooray!

7:30 a.m. Our leader built a fire and cooked eggs over it. We had a delicious breakfast.

8:30 a.m. After doing the dishes, we groomed and tacked up the ponies.

9 a.m. We set off on a long ride. Luckily, our camp was near the ocean, so we rode along the shore. We tried riding in the surf, but some of the ponies didn't want to go in!

12:30 p.m. We returned to camp, brushed the ponies over, and turned them out in the field.

1 p.m. Picnic time! We all ate lunch on the grass.

2 p.m. After lunch, we went into the indoor school for a talk about pony care and feeding by a Pony Club official. I had no idea there was so much to learn!

5 p.m. Dinnertime, with ice cream for dessert. Then we cleaned the tack.

6 p.m. We checked the ponies one last time and then went back to our tents and got ready to sleep. It was supposed to be lights out at 9 p.m., but I was so tired, I was asleep long before that!

Fun at Camp

You will have a great time away at camp, with nothing but ponies to think about. You will spend your whole day riding them and caring for them.

Group Classes

You may have group classes with other riders in a field or an outdoor school. These may be classes in basic riding, or more advanced skills, such as jumping.

Riding for a Day

You may go out on a daylong ride, taking a bag lunch with you. Your pony may wear a halter over its bridle, so you can remove its **bit** and allow it to graze at lunchtime. You will also stop to let it drink when you are near water.

Aftercare

After riding, you will need to take water and food to your pony before you eat your own meal. If it is put in a stable, it will also need hay.

Cleaning the Tack

To make this task more fun, do it with your buddies. First, clean off the grease and any mud with a damp sponge, then rub in saddle soap. Wet the soap, not the sponge, to avoid getting too much foam.

At the end of the day's riding you will need to clean the pony's tack (its saddle and bridle.)

Top Tip!

If you keep your tack clean and supple, it will last for many years.

Competitions

As well as having riding classes, learning how to take care of ponies, and going on long rides, your camp may also hold competitions.

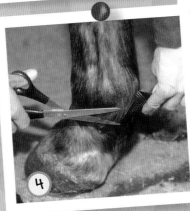

Best Presented Pony
To win this competition, you will need to:

1. Groom your pony until its coat shines.

2. Wash and dry its mane and tail.

3. Wash and dry any white socks.

4. Trim any long hair on its fetlocks.

5. Brush off any mud from its hooves and oil them.

6. Clean the tack.

Best Presented Rider
You will need to look super clean and tidy to win!

Novice Dressage

Your camp may have a **dressage** arena, and they may hold dressage competitions. Even if you're not too good at it, it's great practice for both you and your pony.

This pony is doing a **collected walk**. Ponies may wear wraps on their lower legs when they are working to support their tendons.

These pumpkins make an unusual jump, which some ponies may not like!

Jumping Course

There will probably be a jump course, either of show jumps with colored rails or cross country jumps. Even if you don't compete, you can learn a lot by testing out all the different types of jump.

Team Games

Your riding club or Pony Club center may have a team that competes in games events. If you have a pony that can gallop and turn quickly, and you are good at jumping on and off, you may be able to join the team.

Old Sock Race
In this race, each competitor collects a rolled up sock, gallops down the field, and drops it into a pail. The first team to get all their socks in the pail wins.

Tack Store Race
Here, each member of the team has to pick up an item of tack or grooming equipment, gallop down the field, and drop them into a tray held by another member.

Five Mug Race

The first rider in each team gallops halfway down the field, picks up a mug from a stack upturned on a post, then gallops down the rest of the field to put the mug on top of another post. They then gallop back to the start, and when they get there the second rider sets off. The first team to move all the cups from the first post to the second wins.

Tire Race

In this race a pair of riders race down the field. One jumps off while the other holds her pony, climbs through a tire, then remounts—and the pair gallop back to the start. The first rider dismounts and a third takes her place. The pair gallop off again and the new rider climbs through the tire. This goes on until everyone has taken a turn, and the team to finish first wins.

Stepping Stone Dash

In this race, riders have to vault off their ponies, run along a line of upturned pails, then vault back on again and gallop back to the start.

Glossary

Bit A metal bar that goes in the pony's mouth. It is part of the bridle.

Collected walk A slow walk with short steps. It is used during dressage.

Dressage A competition in which a horse or pony has to carry out precise actions and paces.

Fetlocks The lowest joints in a horse or pony's legs, just above the hooves.

Horse truck A special truck in which horses or ponies are transported.

Horse trailer A type of wagon in which a horse or pony travels. It is pulled by a car.

Longeing To exercise a horse or pony on a long line that is attached to a special halter. The pony may or may not be ridden at the same time.

Tack The saddle, bridle, and other equipment used on a pony when it is being ridden.

Travel boots Protective pads that cover the pony's lower legs to prevent injury when traveling.

Index

Notes for Parents and Teachers

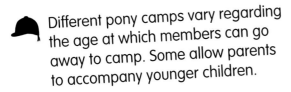

Belonging to The Pony Club or to a local riding club teaches children a lot about ponies and riding that they probably never learn otherwise, especially if their pony is kept at livery—or if they ride a riding school pony. They can find out the answers to all kinds of questions, from pony care to problem solving, and have tuition in all aspects of riding. It's also an opportunity to make new friends and have fun.

Different pony camps vary regarding the age at which members can go away to camp. Some allow parents to accompany younger children.

As far as possible, children will have to take care of their ponies themselves at Pony Club camp. This will give them a real insight into what caring for ponies is all about. They also have to help with all the domestic chores around the camp.

A child does not have to own a pony to belong to a riding club. Some clubs hold meetings at riding schools, so members without ponies of their own can ride the school's ponies. This can be almost as good as having your own pony, as the child will learn how to take care of it, and how to relate to it, as well as how to ride it.

Horse and pony websites

www.ponyclub.org
The Pony Club

www.usef.org
The national governing body for equestrian sport

www.newrider.com
Advice and information for new riders

horseworlddata.com
General information about horses and ponies